PIANO · VOCAL · GUITAR

CHRISTM
SHEET MUSIC
ANTHOLOGY

ISBN 978-1-70514-020-8

Visit Hal Leonard Online at
www.halleonard.com

Contact us:
Hal Leonard
7777 West Bluemound Road
Milwaukee, WI 53213
Email: info@halleonard.com

In Europe, contact:
Hal Leonard Europe Limited
42 Wigmore Street
Marylebone, London, W1U 2RN
Email: info@halleonardeurope.com

In Australia, contact:
Hal Leonard Australia Pty. Ltd.
4 Lentara Court
Cheltenham, Victoria, 3192 Australia
Email: info@halleonard.com.au

Contents

4   All I Want for Christmas Is You

11   All I Want for Christmas Is My Two Front Teeth

14   All Is Well

24   Angels from the Realms of Glory

26   Angels We Have Heard on High

28   Away in a Manger

30   Because It's Christmas (For All the Children)

19   Believe

38   Blue Christmas

40   Break Forth, O Beauteous, Heavenly Light

42   Breath of Heaven (Mary's Song)

50   Bring a Torch, Jeannette, Isabella

52   The Chipmunk Song

54   C-H-R-I-S-T-M-A-S

58   Christmas (Baby Please Come Home)

62   Christmas Eve/Sarajevo 12/24

35   Christmas Is

47   The Christmas Song (Chestnuts Roasting on an Open Fire)

68   Christmas Time Is Here

74   Christmas Vacation

71   The Christmas Waltz

80   Dance of the Sugar Plum Fairy

86   Deck the Hall

81   Do They Know It's Christmas? (Feed the World)

88   Do You Hear What I Hear

94   Feliz Navidad

100   The First Noël

102   The Friendly Beasts

91   Frosty the Snow Man

104   Gesù Bambino (The Infant Jesus)

108   Go, Tell It on the Mountain

110   God Rest Ye Merry, Gentlemen

112   Good King Wenceslas

114   Grandma Got Run Over by a Reindeer

118   Grown-Up Christmas List

97   Happy Holiday

126   Happy Xmas (War Is Over)

130   Hark! The Herald Angels Sing

132   Have Yourself a Merry Little Christmas

138   Here Comes Santa Claus (Right Down Santa Claus Lane)

140   The Holly and the Ivy

123   A Holly Jolly Christmas

142   (There's No Place Like) Home for the Holidays

150   I Heard the Bells on Christmas Day

147   I Saw Mommy Kissing Santa Claus

155   I Wonder as I Wander

152   I'll Be Home for Christmas

158   In the Bleak Midwinter

160   Infant Holy, Infant Lowly

163	It Came Upon the Midnight Clear	250	O Holy Night
166	It Must Have Been the Mistletoe (Our First Christmas)	254	O Little Town of Bethlehem
177	It's Beginning to Look Like Christmas	256	River
172	It's Christmas in New York	266	Rockin' Around the Christmas Tree
180	Jingle Bell Rock	272	Rudolph the Red-Nosed Reindeer
183	Jingle Bells	276	Santa Baby
186	Jingle, Jingle, Jingle	269	Santa Claus Is Comin' to Town
196	Jolly Old St. Nicholas	280	Santa Tell Me
198	Joy to the World	286	Silent Night
200	Let It Snow! Let It Snow! Let It Snow!	288	Silver and Gold
189	Light of the World	290	Silver Bells
202	The Little Drummer Boy	294	Sleigh Ride
212	Little Saint Nick	300	Someday at Christmas
216	Lo, How a Rose E'er Blooming	308	Somewhere in My Memory
207	Mary, Did You Know?	318	Still, Still, Still
218	Mary's Little Boy Child	305	The Twelve Days of Christmas
224	Mele Kalikimaka	320	Ukrainian Bell Carol
221	Merry Christmas, Darling	311	Underneath the Tree
227	Mister Santa	322	Up on the Housetop
241	Mistletoe	324	We Three Kings of Orient Are
230	Mistletoe and Holly	326	We Wish You a Merry Christmas
232	The Most Wonderful Time of the Year	329	What Child Is This?
238	Nuttin' for Christmas	332	Where Are You Christmas?
246	O Christmas Tree	338	While Shepherds Watched Their Flocks
248	O Come, All Ye Faithful	340	White Christmas
263	O Come, O Come, Emmanuel	349	Winter Wonderland
		344	Wonderful Christmastime

ALL I WANT FOR CHRISTMAS IS YOU

Words and Music by MARIAH CAREY
and WALTER AFANASIEFF

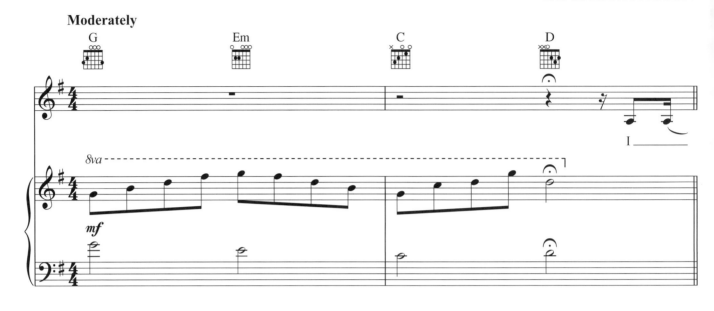

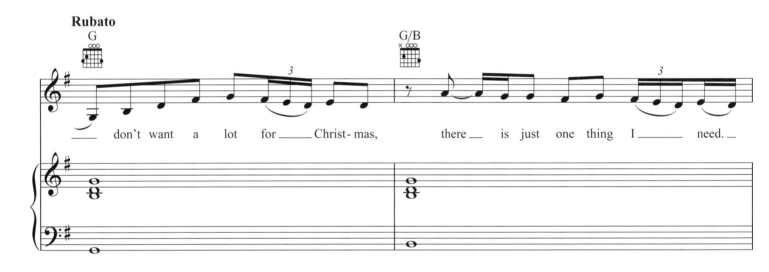

don't want a lot for _____ Christ-mas, there _____ is just one thing I _____ need. _____

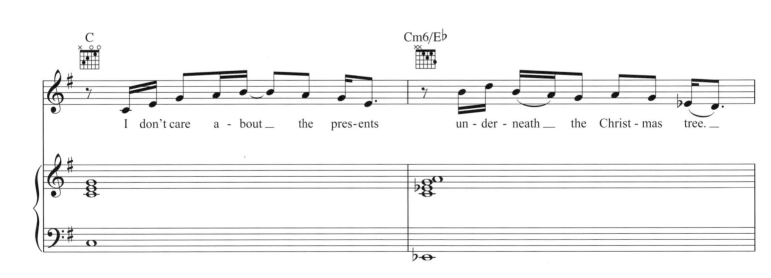

I don't care a-bout _____ the pres-ents un-der-neath _____ the Christ-mas tree. _____

ALL I WANT FOR CHRISTMAS IS MY TWO FRONT TEETH

Words and Music by
DON GARDNER

Brightly

Ev - 'ry - bod - y stops and stares at me. ____

These two teeth are gone as you can see. ____

I don't know just who to blame for this ca - tas - tro - phe! But

ALL IS WELL

Words and Music by MICHAEL W. SMITH
and WAYNE KIRKPATRICK

BELIEVE
from Warner Bros. Pictures' THE POLAR EXPRESS

Words and Music by GLEN BALLARD
and ALAN SILVESTRI

ANGELS FROM THE REALMS OF GLORY

Words by JAMES MONTGOMERY
Music by HENRY T. SMART

An-gels from the realms of glo-ry, Wing your flight o'er all the earth. Ye who sang cre-a-tion's sto-ry, Now pro-claim Mes-si-ah's birth. Come and wor-ship!

ANGELS WE HAVE HEARD ON HIGH

Traditional French Carol
Translated by JAMES CHADWICK

AWAY IN A MANGER

Traditional
Music by JAMES R. MURRAY

A-way in a man-ger, no crib for a bed, The lit-tle Lord Je-sus laid down His sweet head. The stars in the sky ___ looked down where He lay, The lit-tle Lord Je-sus, a-

BECAUSE IT'S CHRISTMAS
(For All the Children)

Music by BARRY MANILOW
Lyric by BRUCE SUSSMAN and JACK FELDMAN

CHRISTMAS IS

Lyrics by SPENCE MAXWELL
Music by PERCY FAITH

BLUE CHRISTMAS

Words and Music by BILLY HAYES
and JAY JOHNSON

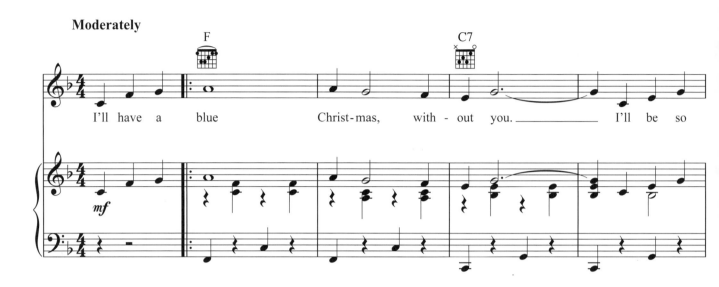

I'll have a blue Christ-mas, with-out you. ___ I'll be so

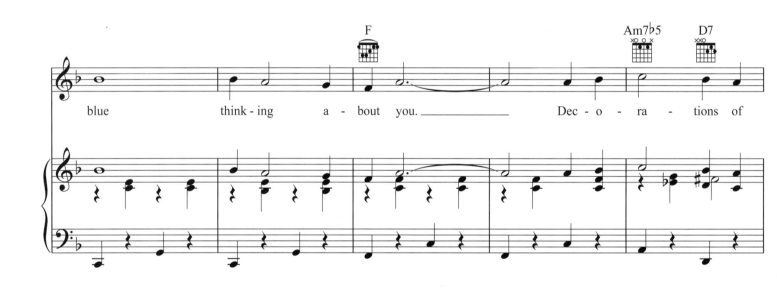

blue think-ing a-bout you. ___ Dec-o-ra-tions of

red on a green Christ-mas tree won't mean a thing if

BREAK FORTH,
O BEAUTEOUS, HEAVENLY LIGHT

Words by JOHANN RIST
Translated by REV. J. TROUTBECK
Melody by JOHANN SCHOP
Arranged by J.S. BACH

BREATH OF HEAVEN
(Mary's Song)

Words and Music by AMY GRANT
and CHRIS EATON

Rubato

Slowly

trav - eled ___ man - y moon - less ___ nights, ___ cold and
wait - ing ___ in a si - lent ___ pray'r. ___ I am
won - der ___ as You watch my ___ face, ___ if a

I have

wea - ry ___ with a babe in - side. ___ And I
fright - ened ___ by the load I ___ bear. ___ In a
wis - er ___ one should have had my ___ place? But I

THE CHRISTMAS SONG
(Chestnuts Roasting on an Open Fire)

Music and Lyric by MEL TORMÉ
and ROBERT WELLS

BRING A TORCH, JEANNETTE, ISABELLA

17th Century French Provençal Carol

Brightly

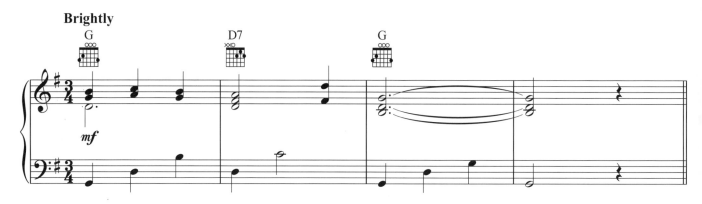

Bring a torch, _____ Jean - nette, Is - a - bel - la,
Has - ten now, _____ good folk of the vil - lage,

Bring a torch, _____ come swift - ly and run.
Has - ten now, _____ the Christ Child to see.

THE CHIPMUNK SONG

Words and Music by
ROSS BAGDASARIAN

C-H-R-I-S-T-M-A-S

Words by JENNY LOU CARSON
Music by EDDY ARNOLD

CHRISTMAS
(Baby Please Come Home)

Words and Music by PHIL SPECTOR,
ELLIE GREENWICH and JEFF BARRY

CHRISTMAS EVE/SARAJEVO 12/24

Music by PAUL O'NEILL
and ROBERT KINKEL

CHRISTMAS TIME IS HERE

from A CHARLIE BROWN CHRISTMAS

Words by LEE MENDELSON
Music by VINCE GUARALDI

THE CHRISTMAS WALTZ

Words by SAMMY CAHN
Music by JULE STYNE

CHRISTMAS VACATION
from NATIONAL LAMPOON'S CHRISTMAS VACATION

Words and Music by BARRY MANN
and CYNTHIA WEIL

Lyrics:

It's that ___ time; Christ-mas time ___ is here.
This old ___ house sure is look - in' good.

Ev - 'ry-bod - y knows ___ there's not a bet - ter time ___ of year.
Got our-selves ___ the fin - est snow-man in the neigh - bor-hood.

DANCE OF THE SUGAR PLUM FAIRY
from THE NUTCRACKER SUITE, OP. 71A

By PYOTR IL'YICH TCHAIKOVSKY

DO THEY KNOW IT'S CHRISTMAS?
(Feed the World)

Words and Music by BOB GELDOF
and MIDGE URE

It's Christ-mas-time, there's no need to be a-fraid.

At Christ-mas-time, we let in light and we ban-ish shade.

And in our world of plen-ty we can spread a smile of joy.

DECK THE HALL

Traditional Welsh Carol

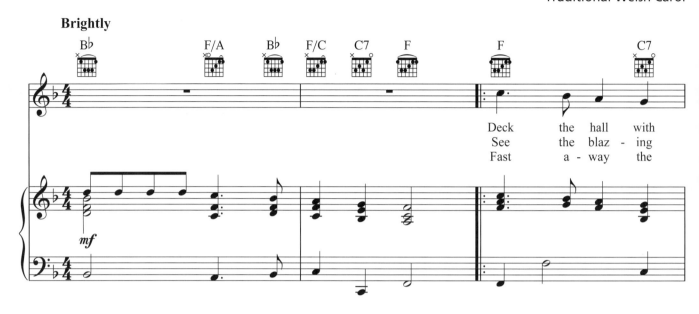

Deck the hall with
See the blaz - ing
Fast a - way the

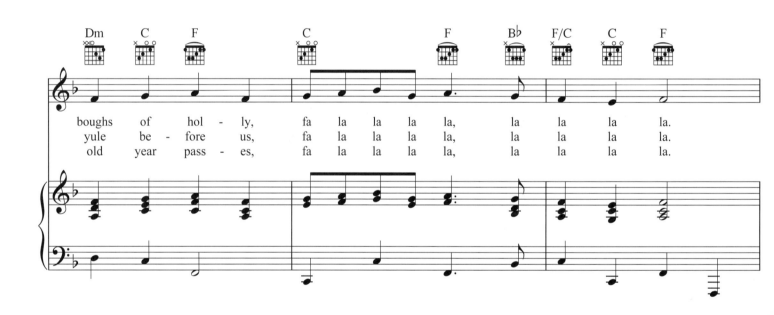

boughs of hol - ly, fa la la la la, la la la la.
yule be - fore us, fa la la la la, la la la la.
old year pass - es, fa la la la la, la la la la.

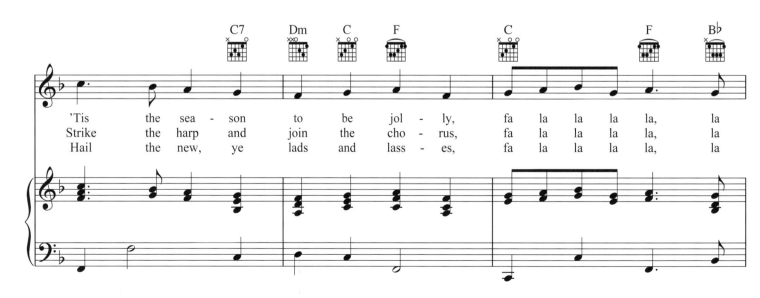

'Tis the sea - son to be jol - ly, fa la la la la, la
Strike the harp and join the cho - rus, fa la la la la, la
Hail the new, ye lads and lass - es, fa la la la la, la

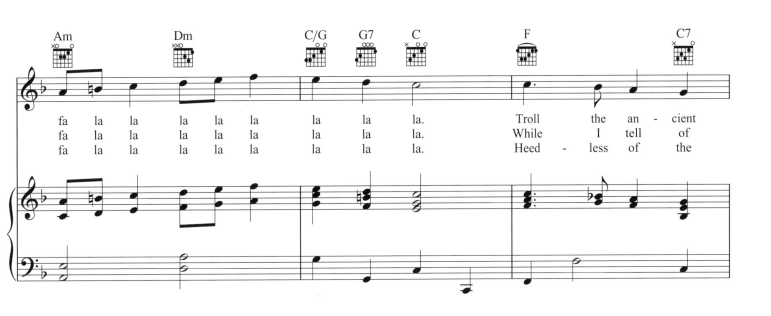

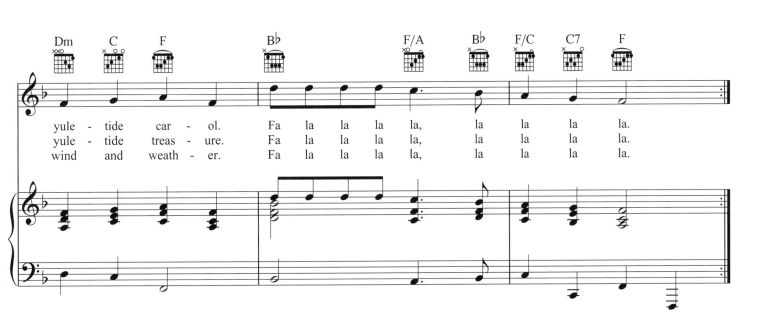

DO YOU HEAR WHAT I HEAR

Words and Music by NOEL REGNEY
and GLORIA SHAYNE

FROSTY THE SNOW MAN

Words and Music by STEVE NELSON
and JACK ROLLINS

FELIZ NAVIDAD

Music and Lyrics by
JOSÉ FELICIANO

Fe - liz Na - vi - dad. _____ Fe - liz Na - vi -

dad. _____ Fe - liz Na - vi - dad. Prós - pe - ro

HAPPY HOLIDAY

from the Motion Picture Irving Berlin's HOLIDAY INN

Words and Music by
IRVING BERLIN

mer - ry bells keep ring - ing, may your ev - 'ry wish come

true. Hap - py hol - i - day, _____ hap - py

hol - i - day. _____ May the cal - en - dar keep

bring - ing hap - py hol - i - days to you.

THE FIRST NOËL

17th Century English Carol
Music from W. Sandys' *Christmas Carols*

Moderately

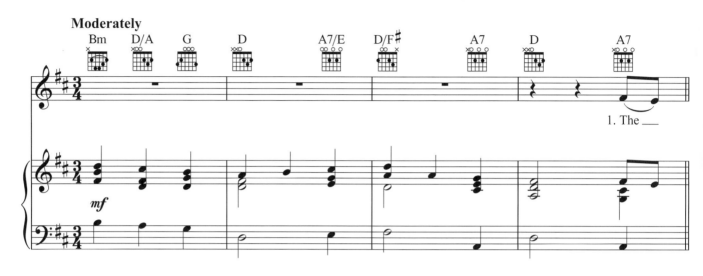

1. The ___

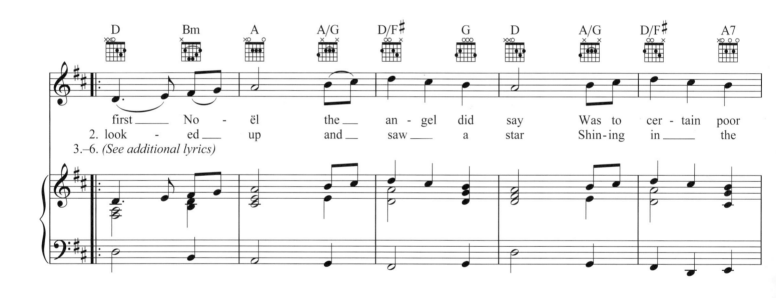

first ___ No - ël the ___ an - gel did say Was to cer - tain poor
2. look - ed ___ up and ___ saw ___ a star Shin - ing in ___ the
3.–6. *(See additional lyrics)*

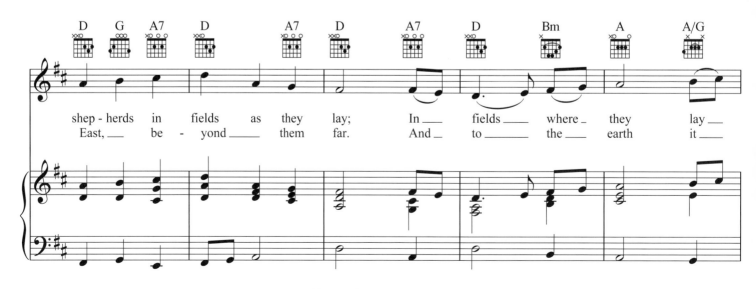

shep - herds in fields as they lay; In ___ fields ___ where ___ they lay ___
East, ___ be - yond ___ them far. And ___ to ___ the ___ earth it

Additional Lyrics

3. And by the light of that same star,
Three wise men came from country far.
To seek for a King was their intent,
And to follow the star wherever it went.
Refrain

4. This star drew nigh to the northwest;
O'er Bethlehem it took its rest.
And there it did both stop and stay,
Right over the place where Jesus lay.
Refrain

5. Then entered in those wise men three,
Full rev'rently upon their knee;
And offered there in His presence,
Their gold and myrrh and frankincense.
Refrain

6. Then let us all with one accord
Sing praises to our heav'nly Lord,
That hath made heav'n and earth of naught,
And with His blood mankind hath bought.
Refrain

THE FRIENDLY BEASTS

Traditional English Carol

Additional Lyrics

2. "I," said the donkey, shaggy and brown,
   "I carried His mother up hill and down;
   I carried her safely to Bethlehem town."
   "I," said the donkey, shaggy and brown.

3. "I," said the cow all white and red,
   "I gave Him my manger for His bed;
   I gave him my hay to pillow His head."
   "I," said the cow all white and red.

4. "I," said the sheep with curly horn,
   "I gave Him my wool for His blanket warm;
   He wore my coat on Christmas morn."
   "I," said the sheep with curly horn.

5. "I," said the dove from the rafters high,
   "I cooed Him to sleep so He would not cry;
   We cooed Him to sleep, my mate and I."
   "I," said the dove from the rafters high.

6. Thus every beast by some good spell,
   In the stable dark was glad to tell
   Of the gift he gave Emmanuel,
   The gift he gave Emmanuel.

GESÙ BAMBINO
(The Infant Jesus)

Text by FREDERICK H. MARTENS
Music by PIETRO YON

GO, TELL IT ON THE MOUNTAIN

African-American Spiritual
Verses by JOHN W. WORK, JR.

GOD REST YE MERRY, GENTLEMEN

19th Century English Carol

God rest ye mer — ry, gen — tle — men, let
Beth — le — hem, in Jew — ry let this
God our Heav'n — ly Fa — ther a

noth — ing you dis — may, For Je — sus Christ our
bless — ed Babe was born, And laid with — in a
bless — ed an — gel came, And un — to cer — tain
joic — ed much in mind, And left to their flocks a —

Sav — ior was born up — on this day, To
man — ger, up — on this bless — ed morn; To
shep — herds brought tid — ings of the same; How
feed — ing in tem — pest, storm and wind; And

GOOD KING WENCESLAS

Words by JOHN M. NEALE
Music from *Piae Cantiones*

With spirit

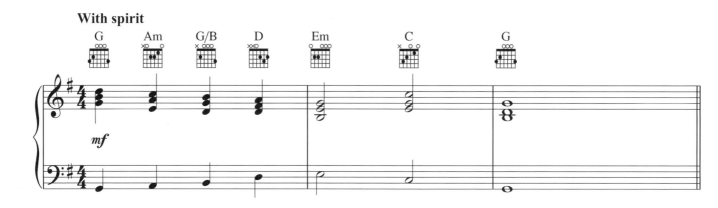

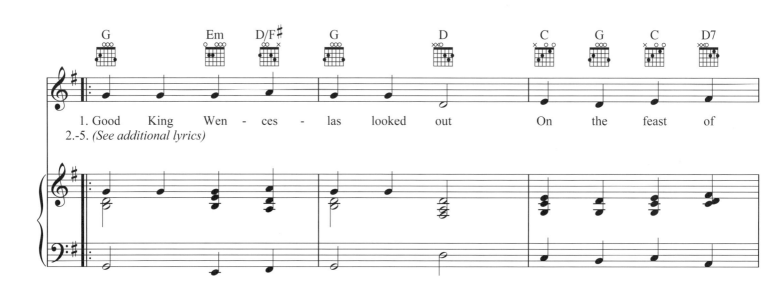

1. Good King Wen - ces - las looked out On the feast of
2.-5. *(See additional lyrics)*

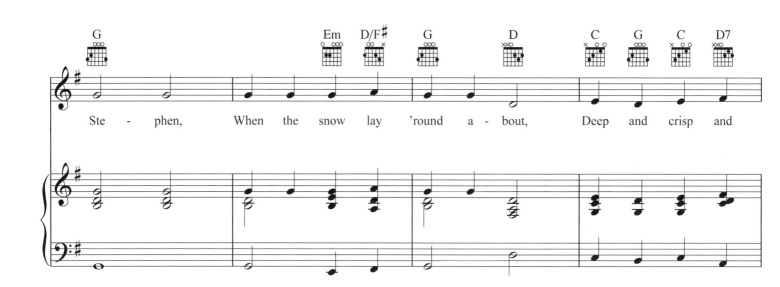

Ste - phen, When the snow lay 'round a - bout, Deep and crisp and

Additional Lyrics

2. "Hither page, and stand by me,
   If thou know'st it, telling,
   Yonder peasant, who is he?
   Where and what his dwelling?"
   "Sire, he lives a good league hence,
   Underneath the mountain;
   Right against the forest fence,
   By Saint Agnes' fountain."

3. "Bring me flesh, and bring me wine,
   Bring me pine-logs hither;
   Thou and I will see him dine,
   When we bear them thither."
   Page and monarch forth they went,
   Forth they went together;
   Through the rude wind's wild lament
   And the bitter weather.

4. "Sire, the night is darker now,
   And the wind blows stronger;
   Fails my heart, I know not how,
   I can go no longer."
   "Mark my footsteps, my good page,
   Tred thou in them boldly:
   Thou shalt find the winter's rage
   Freeze thy blood less coldly."

5. In his master's steps he trod,
   Where the snow lay dinted;
   Heat was in the very sod
   Which the saint had printed.
   Therefore, Christian men, be sure,
   Wealth or rank possessing,
   Ye who now will bless the poor,
   Shall yourselves find blessing.

GRANDMA GOT RUN OVER BY A REINDEER

Words and Music by
RANDY BROOKS

Moderately bright

Grand-ma got run o-ver by a

rein-deer　　walk-ing home from our house Christ-mas Eve.

You can say there's no such thing as San-ta,　　but　as for me and Grand-pa, we be-

You can say there's no such thing as San- ta, but as for me and Grand- pa, we be-

lieve. _____

Additional Lyrics

2. Now we're all so proud of Grandpa,
   He's been taking this so well.
   See him in there watching football,
   Drinking beer and playing cards with Cousin Mel.
   It's not Christmas without Grandma.
   All the family's dressed in black,
   And we just can't help but wonder:
   Should we open up her gifts or send them back?
   Chorus

3. Now the goose is on the table,
   And the pudding made of fig,
   And the blue and silver candles,
   That would just have matched the hair in Grandma's wig.
   I've warned all my friends and neighbors,
   Better watch out for yourselves.
   They should never give a license
   To a man who drives a sleigh and plays with elves.
   Chorus

GROWN-UP CHRISTMAS LIST

Words and Music by DAVID FOSTER
and LINDA THOMPSON-JENNER

And ev - 'ry - one would have a friend, and right would al - ways win, and love would nev - er end. This is my grown - up Christ - mas list.

As list. What is this il - lu - sion called? The in - no - cence of youth. May - be

A HOLLY JOLLY CHRISTMAS

Music and Lyrics by
JOHNNY MARKS

HAPPY XMAS
(War Is Over)

Written by JOHN LENNON
and YOKO ONO

HARK! THE HERALD ANGELS SING

Words by CHARLES WESLEY
Altered by GEORGE WHITEFIELD
Music by FELIX MENDELSSOHN-BARTHOLDY
Arranged by WILLIAM H. CUMMINGS

HAVE YOURSELF A MERRY LITTLE CHRISTMAS

from MEET ME IN ST. LOUIS

Words and Music by HUGH MARTIN
and RALPH BLANE

HERE COMES SANTA CLAUS
(Right Down Santa Claus Lane)

Words and Music by GENE AUTRY
and OAKLEY HALDEMAN

Bells are ring - ing, chil - dren sing - ing, all is mer - ry and
Hear those sleigh - bells jin - gle jan - gle, what a beau - ti - ful
San - ta knows that we're God's chil - dren; that makes ev - 'ry - thing
Peace on earth will come to all if we just fol - low the

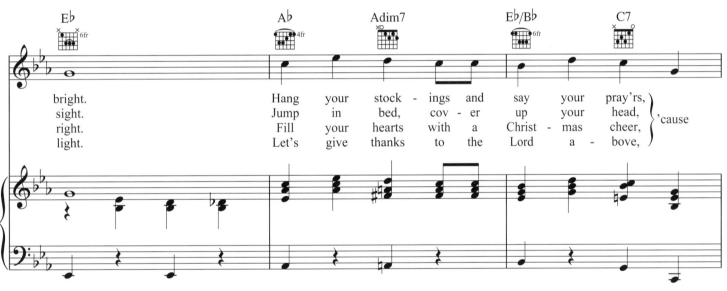

bright.
sight.
right.
light.

Hang your stock - ings and say your pray'rs, }
Jump in bed, cov - er up your head, } 'cause
Fill your hearts with a Christ - mas cheer,
Let's give thanks to the Lord a - bove,

1-3
San - ta Claus comes to - night.

4
San - ta Claus comes to - night.

THE HOLLY AND THE IVY

18th Century English Carol

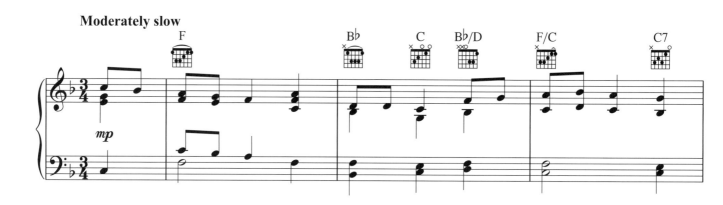

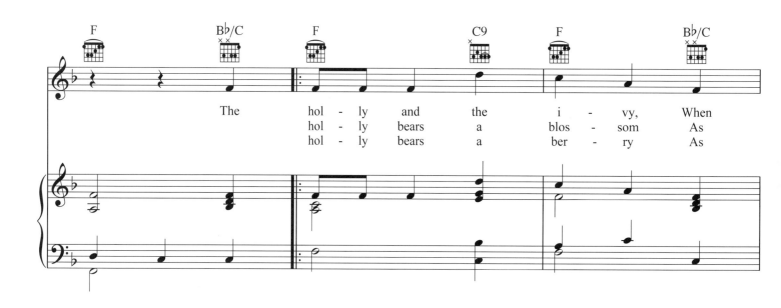

The hol - ly and the i - vy, When
hol - ly bears a blos - som As
hol - ly bears a ber - ry As

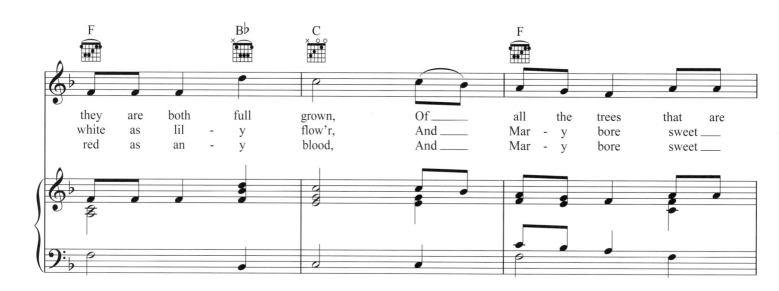

they are both full grown, Of_____ all the trees that are
white as lil - y flow'r, And_____ Mar - y bore sweet_____
red as an - y blood, And_____ Mar - y bore sweet_____

(There's No Place Like)
HOME FOR THE HOLIDAYS

Words and Music by AL STILLMAN
and ROBERT ALLEN

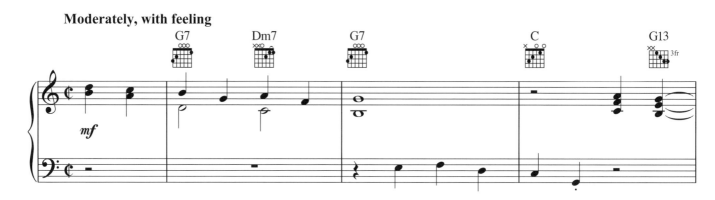

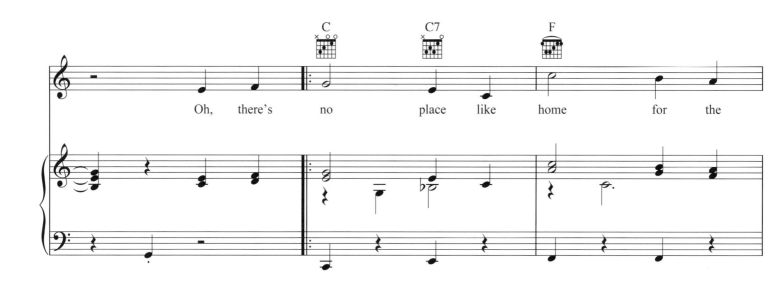

Oh, there's no place like home for the

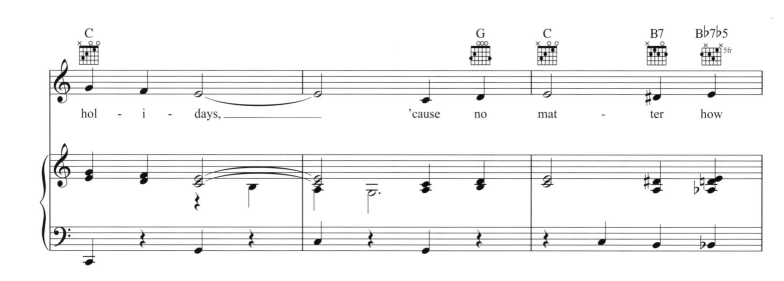

hol-i-days, _____ 'cause no mat-ter how

I SAW MOMMY KISSING SANTA CLAUS

Words and Music by
TOMMIE CONNOR

I HEARD THE BELLS ON CHRISTMAS DAY

Words by HENRY WADSWORTH LONGFELLOW
Adapted by JOHNNY MARKS
Music by JOHNNY MARKS

I'LL BE HOME FOR CHRISTMAS

Words and Music by KIM GANNON
and WALTER KENT

I WONDER AS I WANDER

By JOHN JACOB NILES

IN THE BLEAK MIDWINTER

Poem by CHRISTINA ROSSETTI
Music by GUSTAV HOLST

INFANT HOLY, INFANT LOWLY

Traditional Polish Carol
Paraphrased by EDITH M.G. REED

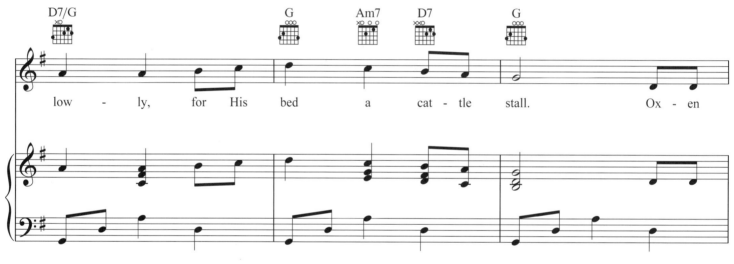

IT CAME UPON THE MIDNIGHT CLEAR

Words by EDMUND HAMILTON SEARS
Music by RICHARD STORRS WILLIS

1. It came up - on ___ the mid - night
2. through the clo - ven skies they
3. with the woes ___ of sin and
4.,5. *(See additional lyrics)*

clear, That glo - rious song ___ of old, ___
come, With peace - ful wings ___ un - furled. ___
strife, The world ___ hath suf - fered long. ___

Additional Lyrics

4. And ye, beneath life's crushing load,
   Whose forms are bending low,
   Who toil along the climbing way
   With painful steps and slow,
   Look now! for glad and golden hours
   Come swiftly on the wing.
   O rest beside the weary road,
   And hear the angels sing.

5. For lo! the days are hast'ning on,
   By prophet-bards foretold.
   When, with the ever-circling years,
   Shall come the Age of Gold,
   When peace shall over all the earth
   Its heav'nly splendors fling,
   And all the world give back the song
   Which now the angels sing.

IT MUST HAVE BEEN THE MISTLETOE
(Our First Christmas)

Words and Music by JUSTIN WILDE
and DOUG KONECKY

IT'S CHRISTMAS IN NEW YORK

Words and Music by
WILLIAM BUTT

IT'S BEGINNING TO LOOK LIKE CHRISTMAS

By MEREDITH WILLSON

JINGLE BELL ROCK

Words and Music by JOE BEAL
and JIM BOOTHE

JINGLE BELLS

Words and Music by
J. PIERPONT

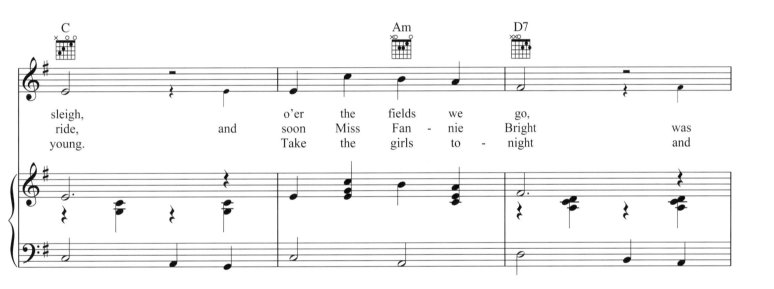

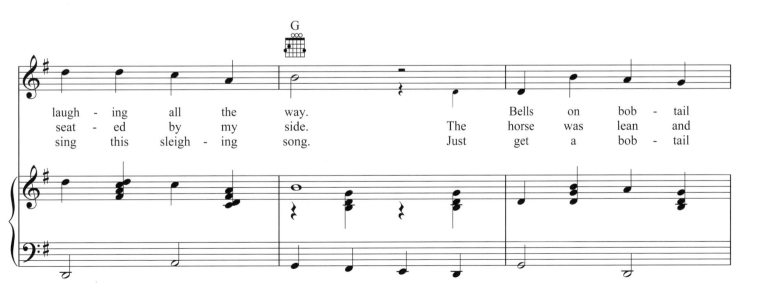

JINGLE, JINGLE, JINGLE

Music and Lyrics by
JOHNNY MARKS

LIGHT OF THE WORLD

Words and Music by LAUREN DAIGLE,
PAUL MABURY and PAUL DUNCAN

Recorded a half step lower.

JOLLY OLD ST. NICHOLAS

Traditional 19th Century American Carol

Brightly

Jol - ly old Saint
When the clock is

Nich - o - las, lean your ear this way. Don't you tell a sin - gle soul
strik - ing twelve, when I'm fast a - sleep, down the chim - ney, broad and black,

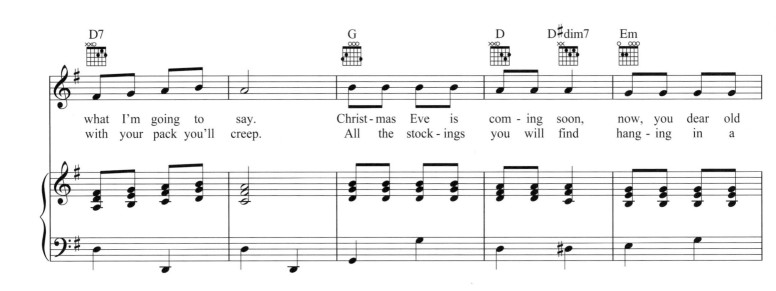

what I'm going to say. Christ - mas Eve is com - ing soon, now, you dear old
with your pack you'll creep. All the stock - ings you will find hang - ing in a

JOY TO THE WORLD

Words by ISAAC WATTS
Music by GEORGE FRIDERIC HANDEL
Adapted by LOWELL MASON

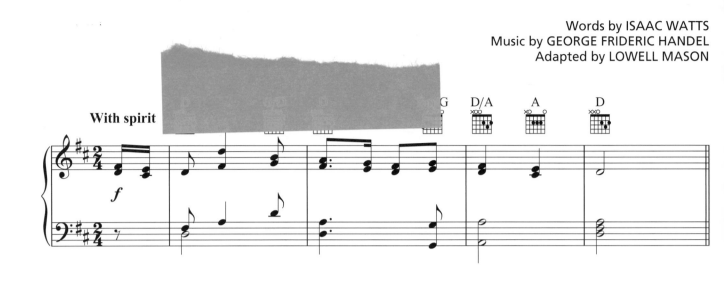

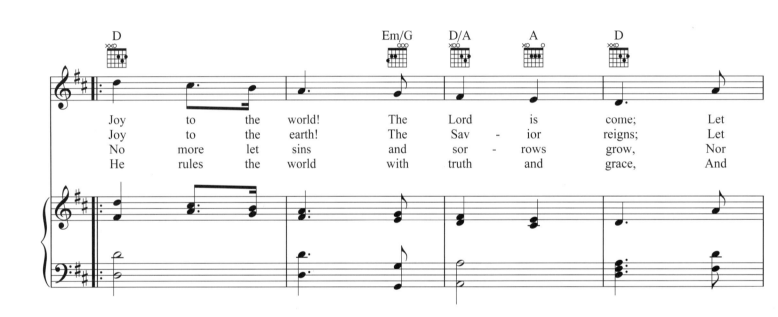

Joy to the world! The Lord is come; Let
Joy to the world! The earth! The Sav - ior reigns; Let
No more let sins and sor - rows grow, Nor
He rules the world with truth and grace, And

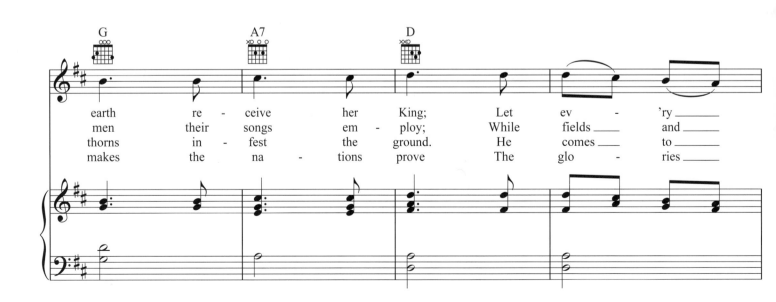

earth re - ceive her King; Let ev - 'ry _____
men their songs em - ploy; While fields _____ and _____
thorns in - fest the ground. He comes _____ to _____
makes the na - tions prove The glo - ries _____

heart ___ pre - pare ___ Him ___ room, ___ and heav'n and na - ture ___
floods, ___ rocks, hills ___ and ___ plains ___ Re - peat the sound - ing ___
make ___ His bless - ings ___ flow ___ Far as the curse is ___
of ___ His right - eous - ness ___ And won - ders of His ___

sing, ___ And ___ heav'n and na - ture ___ sing, ___ And ___
joy, ___ Re - peat the sound - ing ___ joy, ___ Re -
found, ___ Far ___ as the curse is ___ found, ___ Far ___
love, ___ And ___ won - ders of His ___ love, ___ And ___

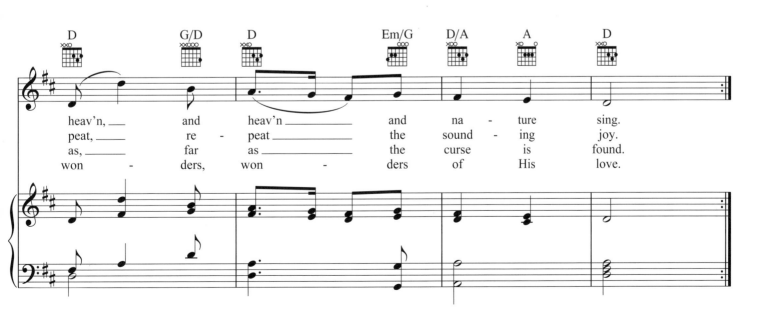

heav'n, ___ and heav'n ___ and na - ture sing.
peat, ___ re - peat ___ the sound - ing joy.
as, ___ far as ___ the curse is found.
won - ders, won - ders of His love.

LET IT SNOW! LET IT SNOW! LET IT SNOW!

Words by SAMMY CAHN
Music by JULE STYNE

THE LITTLE DRUMMER BOY

Words and Music by HARRY SIMEONE,
HENRY ONORATI and KATHERINE DAVIS

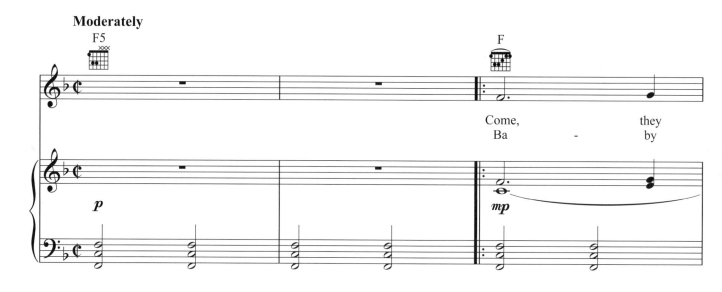

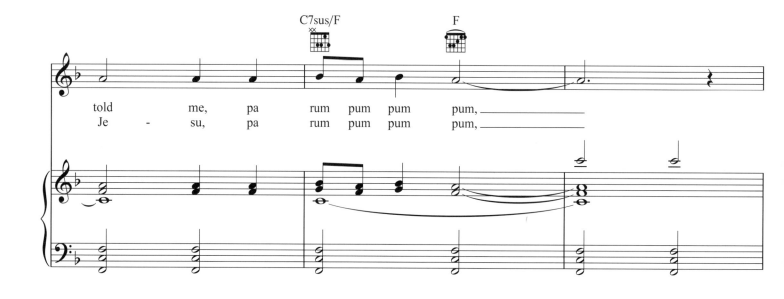

MARY, DID YOU KNOW?

Words and Music by MARK LOWRY
and BUDDY GREENE

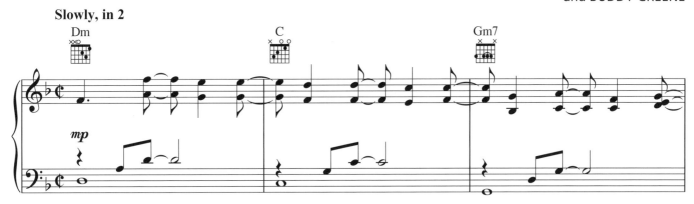

Mar - y, did you know that your ba -

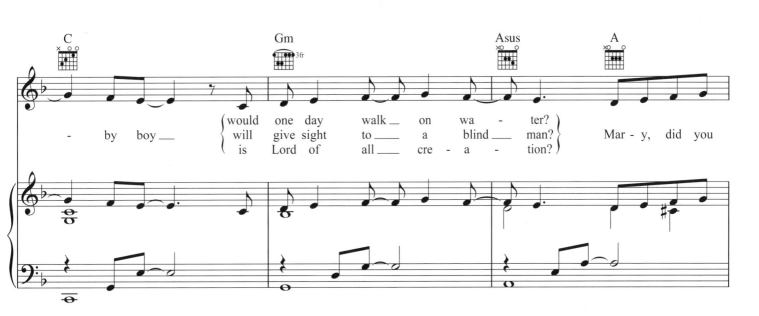

- by boy __

(would one day walk __ on wa - ter?)
will give sight to __ a blind __ man?
is Lord of all __ cre - a - tion?

Mar - y, did you

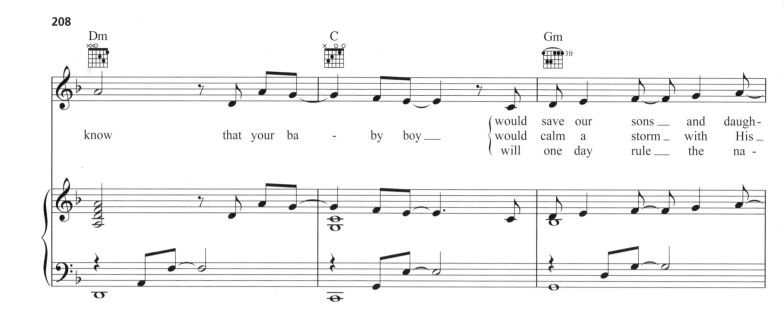

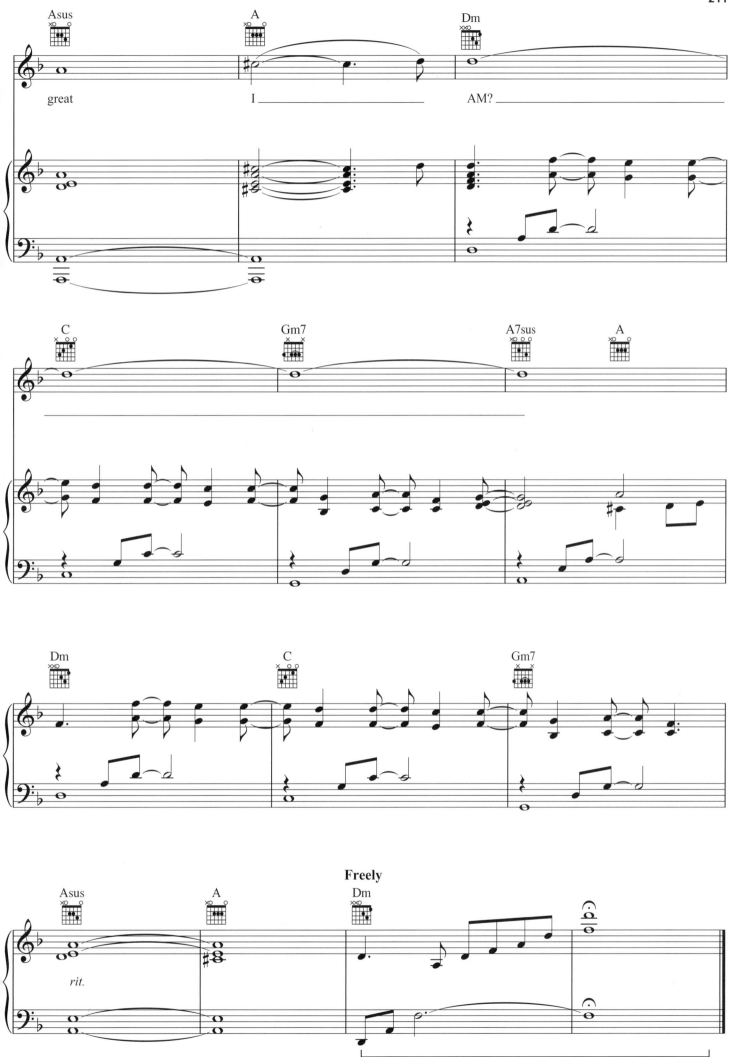

LITTLE SAINT NICK

Words and Music by BRIAN WILSON
and MIKE LOVE

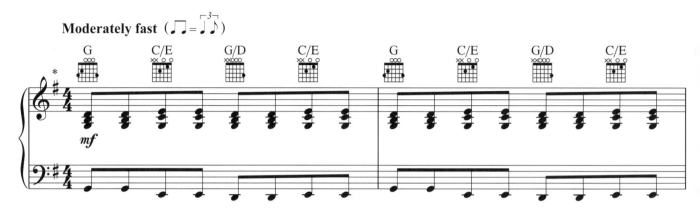

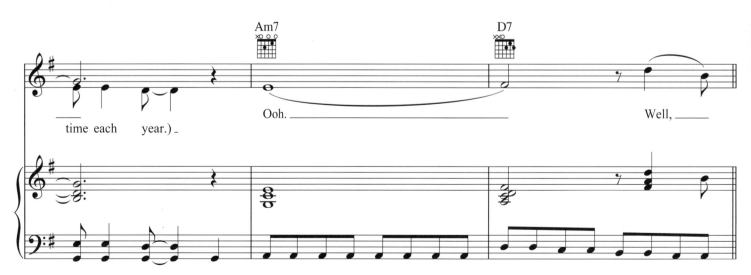

Recorded a half step lower.

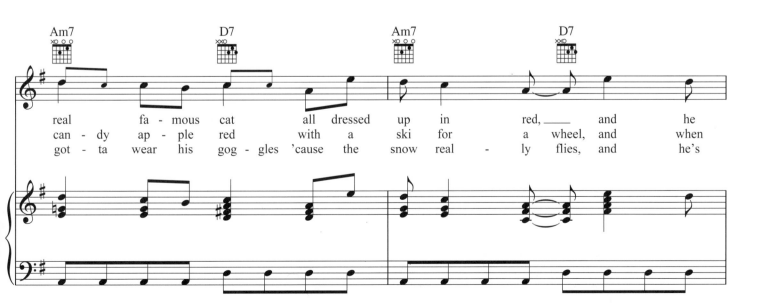

LO, HOW A ROSE E'ER BLOOMING

15th Century German Carol
Translated by THEODORE BAKER
Music from *Alte Catholische Geistliche Kirchengesang*

Tenderly

Lo, how a rose e'er bloom- ing From ten-der stem _____ hath sprung! Of Jes-se's lin-eage com - ing As men of old _____ have sung. It came, a flow'r-et bright, A-mid the cold of win-

MARY'S LITTLE BOY CHILD

Words and Music by
JESTER HAIRSTON

MERRY CHRISTMAS, DARLING

Words and Music by RICHARD CARPENTER
and FRANK POOLER

Greet-ing cards have all been sent, the Christ-mas rush is through,

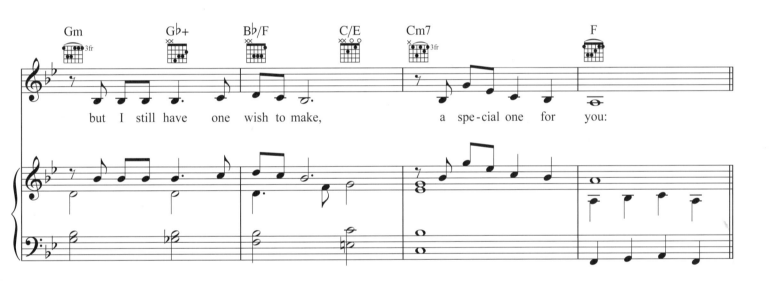

but I still have one wish to make, a spe-cial one for you:

Mer-ry Christ-mas, dar-ling. We're a-part, that's true; but

MELE KALIKIMAKA

Words and Music by
R. ALEX ANDERSON

"Jin - gle Bells" up - on a steel gui - tar;

through the palms we see the same bright star.

Me - le Ka - li - ki - ma - ka is the thing to say _____ on a

MISTER SANTA

Words and Music by
PAT BALLARD

Additional Lyrics

2. Mister Santa, dear old Saint Nick,
   Be awful careful and please don't get sick.
   Put on your coat when breezes are blowin',
   And when you cross the street look where you're goin'.
   Santa, we (I) love you so,
   We (I) hope you never get lost in the snow.
   Take your time when you unpack,
   Mister Santa, don't hurry back.

3. Mister Santa, we've been so good;
   We've washed the dishes and done what we should.
   Made up the beds and scrubbed up our toesies,
   We've used a kleenex when we've blown our nosesies.
   Santa, look at our ears, they're clean as whistles,
   We're sharper than shears.
   Now we've put you on the spot,
   Mister Santa, bring us a lot.

MISTLETOE AND HOLLY

Words and Music by FRANK SINATRA,
DOK STANFORD and HENRY W. SANICOLA

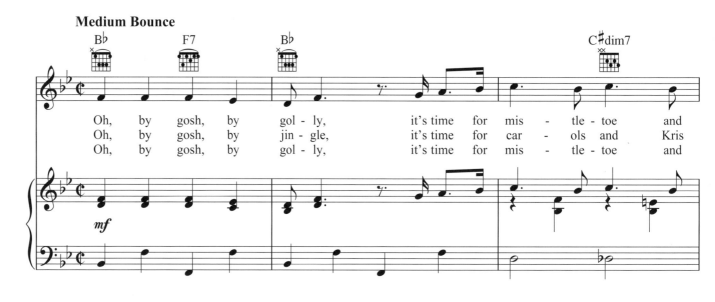

Oh, by gosh, by gol - ly, it's time for mis - tle - toe and
Oh, by gosh, by jin - gle, it's time for car - ols and Kris
Oh, by gosh, by gol - ly, it's time for mis - tle - toe and

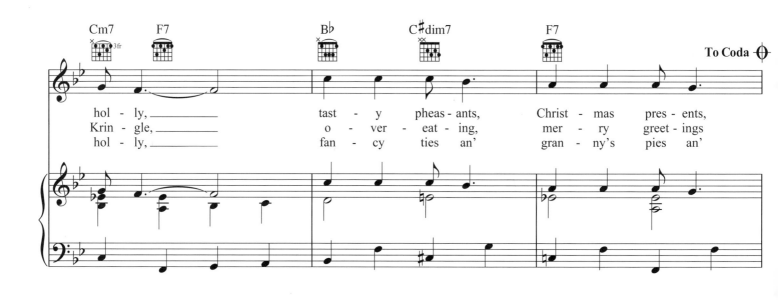

hol - ly, _____ tast - y pheas - ants, Christ - mas pres - ents,
Krin - gle, _____ o - ver - eat - ing, mer - ry greet - ings
hol - ly, _____ fan - cy ties an' gran - ny's pies an'

coun - try-sides cov - ered with snow.
from ___ rel - a - tives you don't know.

THE MOST WONDERFUL
TIME OF THE YEAR

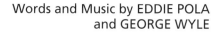

Words and Music by EDDIE POLA
and GEORGE WYLE

all. _____ There'll be par - ties for

host - ing, marsh - mal - lows for toast - ing and car - ol - ing out in the

snow. There'll be scar - y ghost sto - ries and tales of the

glo - ries of Christ - mas - es long, long a - go. _____ It's the

D.S. al Coda

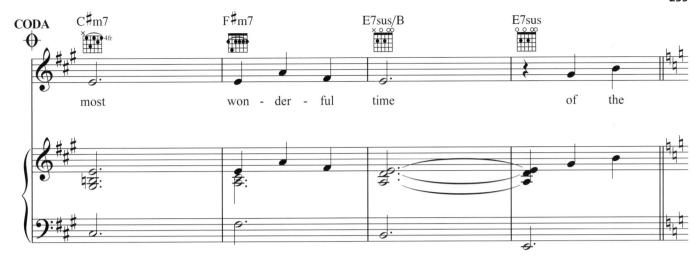

most won-der-ful time of the

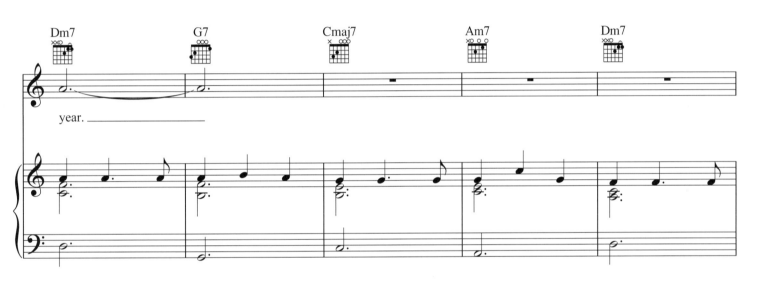

year.

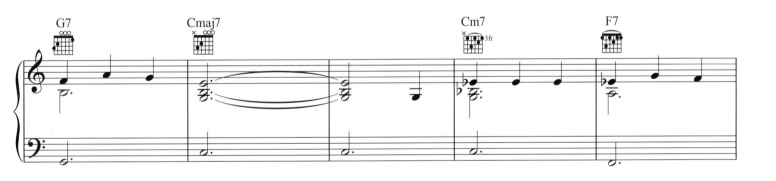

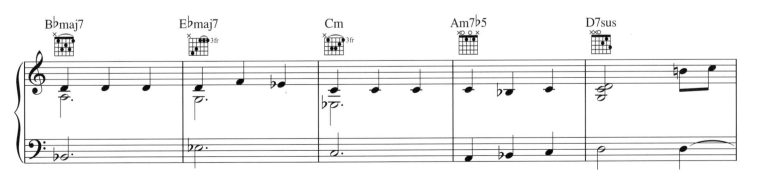

NUTTIN' FOR CHRISTMAS

Words and Music by ROY C. BENNETT
and SID TEPPER

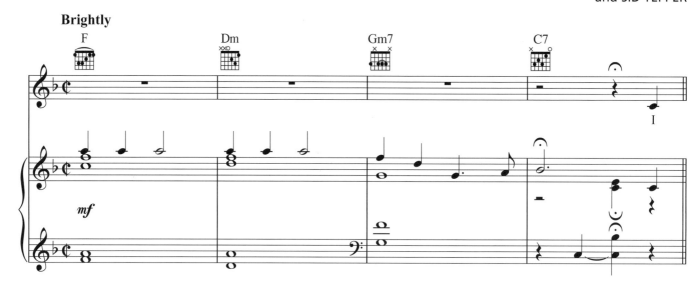

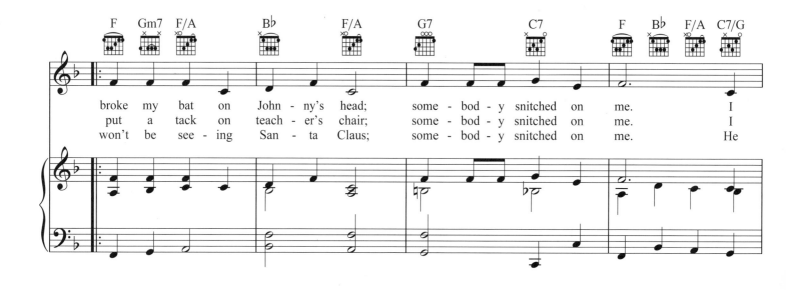

broke my bat on John - ny's head; some - bod - y snitched on me. I
put a tack on teach - er's chair; some - bod - y snitched on me. I
won't be see - ing San - ta Claus; some - bod - y snitched on me. He

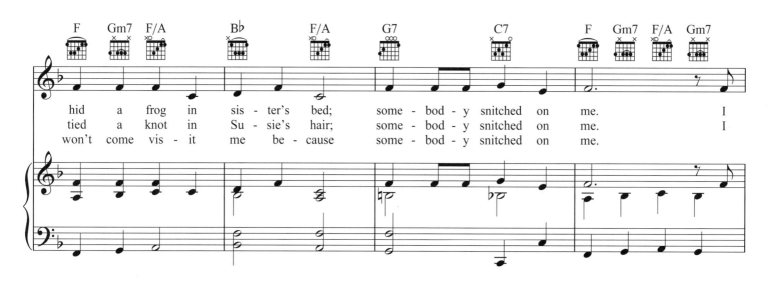

hid a frog in sis - ter's bed; some - bod - y snitched on me. I
tied a knot in Su - sie's hair; some - bod - y snitched on me. I
won't come vis - it me be - cause some - bod - y snitched on me.

MISTLETOE

Words and Music by JUSTIN BIEBER,
NASRI ATWEH and ADAM MESSINGER

O CHRISTMAS TREE

Traditional German Carol

O COME, ALL YE FAITHFUL

Music by JOHN FRANCIS WADE
Latin Words translated by FREDERICK OAKELEY

O HOLY NIGHT

French Words by PLACIDE CAPPEAU
English Words by JOHN S. DWIGHT
Music by ADOLPHE ADAM

Slow and flowing

O ho-ly night, _____ the
Tru - ly He taught us to

stars are bright-ly shin - ing; it is the night of the
love one an - oth - er; His law is love, and His

dear Sav - ior's birth. _____ Long lay the
gos - pel is peace. _____ Chains shall He

O LITTLE TOWN OF BETHLEHEM

Words by PHILLIPS BROOKS
Music by LEWIS H. REDNER

1. O lit - tle town of Beth - le - hem, How
2. Christ is born of Mar - y, And
3., 4. *(See additional lyrics)*

still we ___ see thee lie! A - bove thy deep and
gath - ered ___ all a - bove, While mor - tals sleep and the

dream - less sleep The si - lent ___ stars go by. Yet
an - gels keep Their watch of ___ won - d'ring love. O

Additional Lyrics

3. How silently, how silently
   The wondrous Gift is giv'n!
   So God imparts to human hearts
   The blessings of His heav'n.
   No ear may hear His coming,
   But in this world of sin,
   Where meek souls will receive Him, still
   The dear Christ enters in.

4. O Holy Child of Bethlehem,
   Descend to us, we pray.
   Cast out our sin, and enter in,
   Be born in us today.
   We hear the Christmas angels
   The great glad tidings tell.
   O come to us, abide with us,
   Our Lord Emmanuel!

RIVER

Words and Music by
JONI MITCHELL

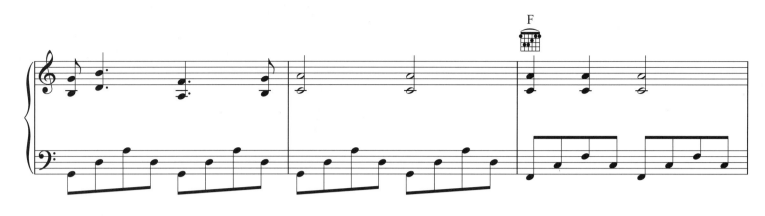

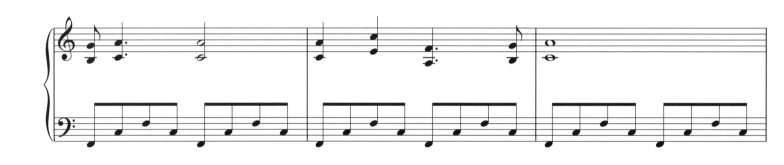

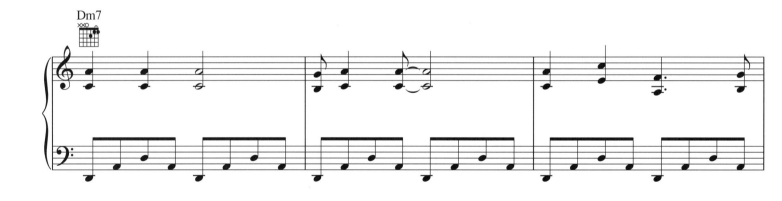

O COME, O COME, EMMANUEL

Traditional Latin Text
15th Century French Melody
Adapted by THOMAS HELMORE

Moderately slow, in 2

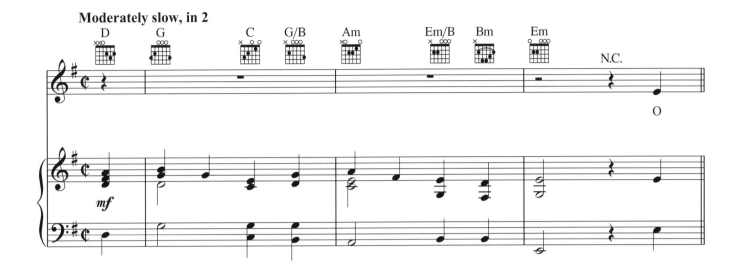

O

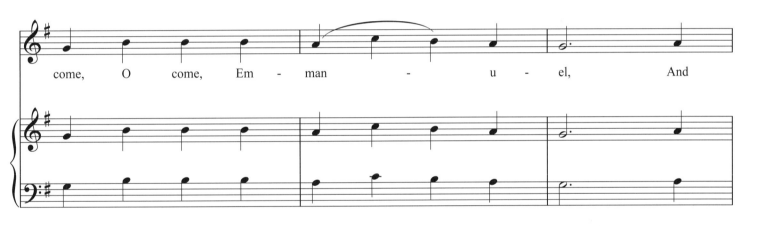

come, O come, Em- man - u - el, And

ran- som cap- tive Is - ra - el, That mourns in lone- ly

ROCKIN' AROUND THE CHRISTMAS TREE

Music and Lyrics by
JOHNNY MARKS

SANTA CLAUS IS COMIN' TO TOWN

Words by HAVEN GILLESPIE
Music by J. FRED COOTS

RUDOLPH THE RED-NOSED REINDEER

Music and Lyrics by
JOHNNY MARKS

SANTA BABY

By JOAN JAVITS,
PHIL SPRINGER and TONY SPRINGER

SANTA TELL ME

Words and Music by SAVAN KOTECHA,
ILYA and ARIANA GRANDE

SILENT NIGHT

Words by JOSEPH MOHR
Translated by JOHN F. YOUNG
Music by FRANZ X. GRUBER

SILVER AND GOLD

Music and Lyrics by
JOHNNY MARKS

SILVER BELLS

from the Paramount Picture THE LEMON DROP KID

Words and Music by JAY LIVINGSTON
and RAY EVANS

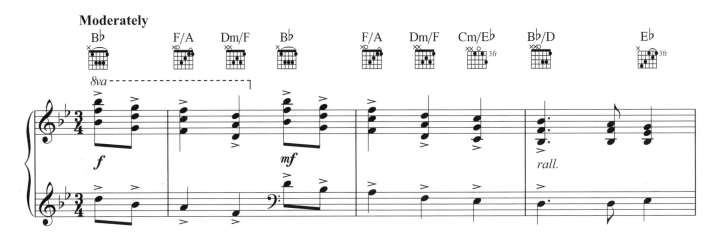

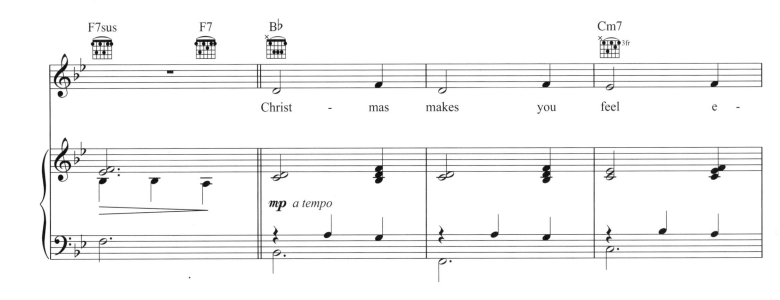

Christ - mas makes you feel e -

mo - tion - al. It may bring par - ties or thoughts de -

SLEIGH RIDE

Music by LEROY ANDERSON
Words by MITCHELL PARISH

SOMEDAY AT CHRISTMAS

Words and Music by RONALD N. MILLER
and BRYAN WELLS

Some-day at Christ-mas men won't be boys,
Some-day at Christ-mas there'll be no wars

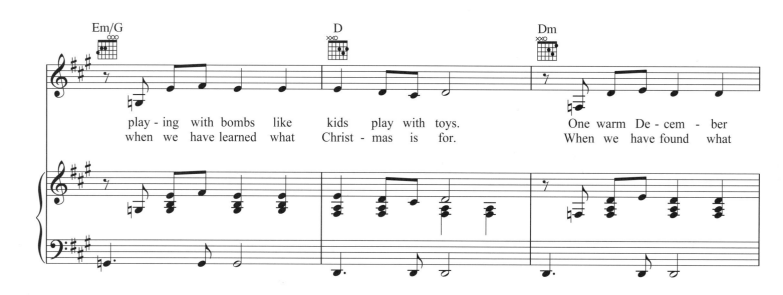

play-ing with bombs like kids play with toys. One warm De-cem-ber
when we have learned what Christ-mas is for. When we have found what

our hearts will see a world where men are _____ free, mm. _____
life's real-ly worth,

THE TWELVE DAYS OF CHRISTMAS

Traditional English Carol

SOMEWHERE IN MY MEMORY

from the Twentieth Century Fox Motion Picture HOME ALONE

Words by LESLIE BRICUSSE
Music by JOHN WILLIAMS

UNDERNEATH THE TREE

Words and Music by KELLY CLARKSON
and GREG KURSTIN

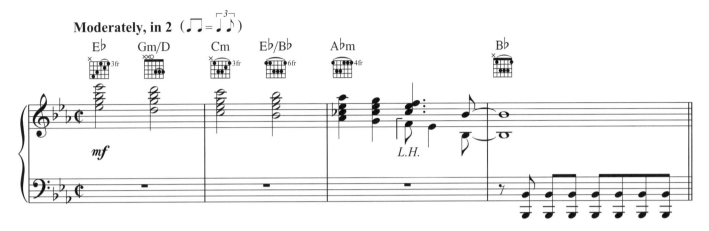

You're here __ where you should be. __ Snow is fall-ing as the

car-ol-ers sing. __ It just was-n't the same __ a-

STILL, STILL, STILL

Salzburg Melody, c.1819
Traditional Austrian Text

Gently

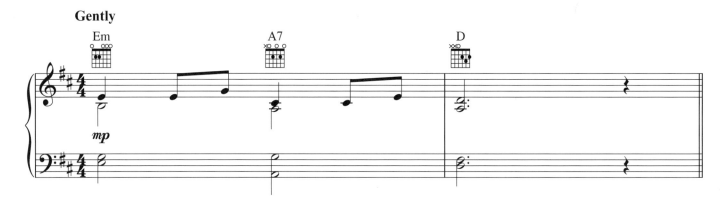

Still, still, still; to sleep is now His
Sleep, sleep, sleep, while we Thy vig - il

will. On Mar - y's breast He rests in slum - ber
keep. And an - gels come He from Heav - en sing - ing

UKRAINIAN BELL CAROL

Traditional
Music by MYKOLA LEONTOVYCH

UP ON THE HOUSETOP

Words and Music by
B.R. HANBY

WE THREE KINGS OF ORIENT ARE

Words and Music by
JOHN H. HOPKINS, JR.

WE WISH YOU A MERRY CHRISTMAS

Traditional English Folksong

WHAT CHILD IS THIS?

Words by WILLIAM C. DIX
16th Century English Melody

WHERE ARE YOU CHRISTMAS?

from DR. SEUSS' HOW THE GRINCH STOLE CHRISTMAS

Words and Music by WILL JENNINGS,
JAMES HORNER and MARIAH CAREY

WHILE SHEPHERDS WATCHED THEIR FLOCKS

Words by NAHUM TATE
Music by GEORGE FRIDERIC HANDEL

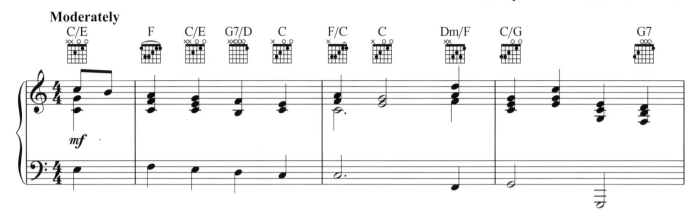

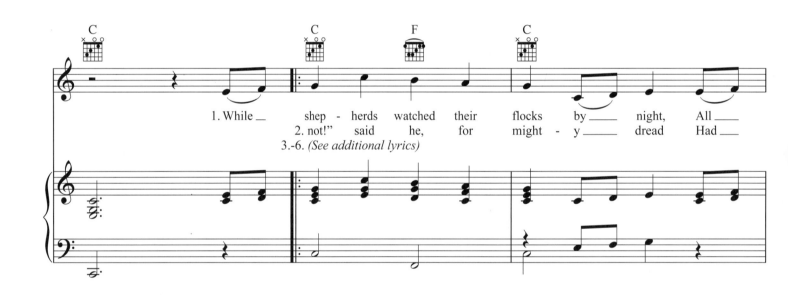

1. While ___ shep-herds watched their flocks by ___ night, All ___
2. not!" said he, for might-y ___ dread All ___
3.-6. *(See additional lyrics)*

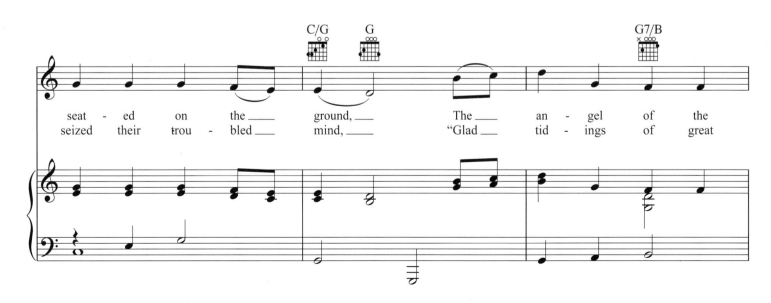

seat-ed on the ___ ground, ___ The ___ an-gel of the
seized their trou-bled ___ mind, ___ "Glad ___ tid-ings of great

Additional Lyrics

3. To you, in David's town this day,
   Is born of David's line,
   The Savior, who is Christ the Lord;
   And this shall be the sign,
   And this shall be the sign:

4. The heavenly Babe you there shall find
   To human view displayed,
   All meanly wrapped in swathing bands,
   And in a manger laid,
   And in a manger laid."

5. Thus spake the seraph; and forthwith
   Appeared a shining throng
   Of angels praising God on high,
   Who thus addressed their song,
   Who thus addressed their song:

6. "All glory be to God on high,
   And to the earth be peace;
   Good will henceforth from heav'n to men,
   Begin and never cease,
   Begin and never cease!"

WHITE CHRISTMAS

from the Motion Picture Irving Berlin's HOLIDAY INN

Words and Music by
IRVING BERLIN

WONDERFUL CHRISTMASTIME

Words and Music by
PAUL McCARTNEY

WINTER WONDERLAND

Words by DICK SMITH
Music by FELIX BERNARD

Sleigh-bells ring; are you lis-t'nin'? In the lane, snow is glis-t'nin'. A beau-ti-ful sight, __ we're hap-py to-night, __ walk-in' in a win-ter won-der-land! Gone a-

CHRISTMAS COLLECTIONS
FROM HAL LEONARD
ALL BOOKS ARRANGED FOR PIANO, VOICE & GUITAR

THE BEST CHRISTMAS SONGS EVER

69 all-time favorites: Auld Lang Syne • Coventry Carol • Frosty the Snow Man • Happy Holiday • It Came Upon the Midnight Clear • O Holy Night • Rudolph the Red-Nosed Reindeer • Silver Bells • What Child Is This? • and many more.

00359130 ....$29.99

THE BIG BOOK OF CHRISTMAS SONGS

Over 120 all-time favorites and hard-to-find classics: As Each Happy Christmas • The Boar's Head Carol • Carol of the Bells • Deck the Halls • The Friendly Beasts • God Rest Ye Merry Gentlemen • Joy to the World • Masters in This Hall • O Holy Night • Story of the Shepherd • and more.

00311520 ....$22.99

CHRISTMAS SONGS – BUDGET BOOKS

100 holiday favorites: All I Want for Christmas Is You • Christmas Time Is Here • Feliz Navidad • Grandma Got Run Over by a Reindeer • I'll Be Home for Christmas • Last Christmas • O Holy Night • Please Come Home for Christmas • Rockin' Around the Christmas Tree • We Need a Little Christmas • What Child Is This? • and more.

00310887 ....$14.99

CHRISTMAS MOVIE SONGS

34 holiday hits from the big screen: All I Want for Christmas Is You • Believe • Christmas Vacation • Do You Want to Build a Snowman? • Frosty the Snow Man • Have Yourself a Merry Little Christmas • It's Beginning to Look like Christmas • Mele Kalikimaka • Rudolph the Red-Nosed Reindeer • Silver Bells • White Christmas • You're a Mean One, Mr. Grinch • and more.

00146961 ....$19.99

CHRISTMAS PIANO SONGS FOR DUMMIES®

56 favorites: Auld Lang Syne • Away in a Manger • Blue Christmas • The Christmas Song • Deck the Hall • I'll Be Home for Christmas • Jingle Bells • Joy to the World • My Favorite Things • Silent Night • more!

00311387 ....$19.95

CHRISTMAS POP STANDARDS

22 contemporary holiday hits, including: All I Want for Christmas Is You • Christmas Time Is Here • Little Saint Nick • Mary, Did You Know? • Merry Christmas, Darling • Santa Baby • Underneath the Tree • Where Are You Christmas? • and more.

00348998 ....$14.99

CHRISTMAS SING-ALONG

40 seasonal favorites: Away in a Manger • Christmas Time Is Here • Feliz Navidad • Happy Holiday • Jingle Bells • Mary, Did You Know? • O Come, All Ye Faithful • Rudolph the Red-Nosed Reindeer • Silent Night • White Christmas • and more. Includes online sing-along backing tracks.

00278176 Book/Online Audio $24.99

CHRISTMAS SONGS FOR KIDS

28 favorite songs of the season, including: Away in a Manger • Do You Want to Build a Snowman? • Here Comes Santa Claus (Right down Santa Claus Lane) • Mele Kalikimaka • Rudolph the Red-Nosed Reindeer • Santa Claus Is Comin' to Town • Silent Night • Somewhere in My Memory • and many more.

00311571 ....$12.99

100 CHRISTMAS CAROLS

Includes: Away in a Manger • Bring a Torch, Jeannette, Isabella • Coventry Carol • Deck the Hall • The First Noel • Go, Tell It on the Mountain • I Heard the Bells on Christmas Day • Joy to the World • O Come, All Ye Faithful (Adeste Fideles) • Silent Night • Sing We Now of Christmas • and more.

00310897 ....$19.99

100 MOST BEAUTIFUL CHRISTMAS SONGS

Includes: Angels We Have Heard on High • Baby, It's Cold Outside • Christmas Time Is Here • Do You Hear What I Hear • Grown-Up Christmas List • Happy Xmas (War Is Over) • I'll Be Home for Christmas • The Little Drummer Boy • Mary, Did You Know? • O Holy Night • White Christmas • Winter Wonderland • and more.

00237285 ....$24.99

POPULAR CHRISTMAS SHEET MUSIC: 1980-2017

40 recent seasonal favorites: All I Want for Christmas Is You • Because It's Christmas (For All the Children) • Breath of Heaven (Mary's Song) • Christmas Lights • The Christmas Shoes • The Gift • Grown-Up Christmas List • Last Christmas • Santa Tell Me • Snowman • Where Are You Christmas? • Wrapped in Red • and more.

00278089 ....$17.99

A SENTIMENTAL CHRISTMAS BOOK

27 beloved Christmas favorites, including: The Christmas Shoes • The Christmas Song (Chestnuts Roasting on an Open Fire) • Christmas Time Is Here • Grown-Up Christmas List • Have Yourself a Merry Little Christmas • I'll Be Home for Christmas • Somewhere in My Memory • Where Are You Christmas? • and more.

00236830 ....$14.99

ULTIMATE CHRISTMAS

100 seasonal favorites: Auld Lang Syne • Bring a Torch, Jeannette, Isabella • Carol of the Bells • The Chipmunk Song • Christmas Time Is Here • The First Noel • Frosty the Snow Man • Gesù Bambino • Happy Holiday • Happy Xmas (War Is Over) • Jingle-Bell Rock • Pretty Paper • Silver Bells • Suzy Snowflake • and more.

00361399 ....$24.99

A VERY MERRY CHRISTMAS

39 familiar favorites: Blue Christmas • Feliz Navidad • Happy Xmas (War Is Over) • I'll Be Home for Christmas • Jingle-Bell Rock • Please Come Home for Christmas • Rockin' Around the Christmas Tree • Santa, Bring My Baby Back (To Me) • Sleigh Ride • White Christmas • and more.

00310536 ....$14.99